AN IMPRINT OF WHAT BOOKS PRESS | LOS ANGELES

ALSO BY HOLADAY MASON

Collections
The "She" Series: A Venice Correspondence
  (with Sarah Maclay)
The Weaver's Body
The Red Bowl: A Fable in Poems
Dissolve
Towards the Forest

Limited Edition Chapbooks
Interlude
Light Spilling from its Own Cup

AS IF
SCATTERED

AS IF SCATTERED

POEMS

Holaday Mason

ISBN: 979-8-9900149-2-3

Library of Congress Control Number: 2024906340

Cover art: Gronk, *Untitled*, 2022
Book design by Ash Good, www.ashgood.com

Giant Claw
363 South Topanga Canyon Boulevard
Topanga, CA 90290

GIANTCLAWPRESS.COM

For Adrian

Be sure to live your life, because
you're a long time dead.

—Scottish Proverb

CONTENTS

BEDTIME STORIES

6	*Bedtime*
7	**A Bedtime Story**
8	*Kiss*
9	**Kiss in an Upstairs Window**
10	*Imagoes*
11	**Imagoes, Minerals**
12	*Slumber*
13	**The Sign Says We Are All Slumber Soon**
14	*Between*
15	**Between One P.M. & Four**
16	*Music*
17	**Old Music**
20	*Chorale*
21	**Neptune Chorale**
22	*Tiny Spears*
23	**And Both of Us Saw Tiny Spears of Violets**
26	*Netsuke*
27	**Netsuke Gradually Waking**
28	*Woman Leaning Over*
29	**Woman Leaning Over a Resting Man Reciting a Myth**
30	*God*
31	**A Wounded God Dressed in Brocade**

HE CARRIES ME LIKE A BOUQUET OF FLOWERS

34	*Lizards*
35	**Lizards Are Always Dreaming**
36	*Overflowing*
37	**The Room Overflowing with Tulips**
38	*At All Hours*
39	**Summoned to Perform at All Hours of the Night**
40	*Tiptoeing*
41	**Tiptoeing**
42	*Always*
43	**Ancient Is Always**
44	*The Sea*
45	**Into the Sea**
46	*Sunlight*
47	**Late Sunlight like Monet**
48	*Chimes*
49	**So What if the Chimes Are Silent?**

EXTINCTION

52	*Ashes*
53	**Talking to Ashes**
54	*Elegy*
55	**Orchard Elegy**

56 *On Fire*

57 No One Dreams We Are on Fire

58 *Covid*

59 A Covid Christmas Card

62 *Wolves*

63 Stone Wolves

64 *Biography*

65 You Need to Get Over Your Biography

66 *Sealed*

67 The Earth Then Sealed

70 *Monster*

71 Monster Considered

72 *Pain*

73 Dear Pain

74 *Extinction*

75 Extinction: The Woman in the Box

76 *Empathy*

77 Empathy Drawn on Asphalt

82 *In a Mirror*

83 A Leaf, A Lagoon in a Mirror / Catskills Autumnal

86 *The Oceans*

87 From the Mountains to the Prairies to the Oceans White With Foam

93 Notes

95 Acknowledgments

BEDTIME STORIES

Look what I become: white flowers, white breasts,
their red nipples the perfect center.

—Holly Prado

Bedtime

We hold

just the essentials,

our limbs more naked.

I open the hymns.

We are a train of lightning.

A Bedtime Story

The body beneath
me is a bellows, a train.

The hymns of our instruments
strike the air, our limbs
a nexus of lightning.

Fluffing the pillows into a street
carnival, we travel from our old selves

carrying just the essentials.
I open. He opens me more.

The oil of laughter melts
the webs around our eyes,

it dampens our hair,
turns us more naked.

We hold each other up
to the native light.

We are translucent. Huge.

Should we be able to see so much?

Kiss

So cautious

they nearly hurt,

agile flames

start

a new alphabet—

shadow lockets

cross our bodies

with every tear of light.

Kiss in an Upstairs Window

Shadow lockets come together
in the folds on the windowsill

where eight lit candles throw
arras of light into the corners.

We decide to give it a try.

The shy drama of silhouettes
that move across our bodies

are restless as a midnight city.

Cautious at the start
of a new alphabet,

our letters to one another
are so tender they hurt.

Agile flames reveal us
& we take part.

We dance with the sycamores.

Imagoes

You reach.

I rise

into the minerals

of our sweat.

Each instant

trembles.

Imagoes, Minerals

How could I not want
to have your rock-star hair
catch under my ribs, twisting
us into pupas as we rest.

Every hour equals loss & gain,
tomorrow the price we all pay—
so please don't shave your silver
chest curls, my home is there,
my nest of found things—

the ordinary growing glossy
& low with August heat as I slip
willingly into the mineral
tang of our sweat.

From the bed I see
the stems of the petite violet
callas you brought have
softened in the green glass vase.
Yet their folds are still
splendid & whole, the way
you lead & I rise to meet you

dazzle to dazzle, the dusty
collections of our years
cast off like outer petals,
as an unexpected calyx unfurls
expanding & so fine-tuned,
I can hear your fingers
tremble as you reach.

Slumber

A strange peace

fills the umbrella

of darkness.

He returns evergreen.

Small glimmers rip the sky.

The Sign Says We Are All Slumber Soon

Such an unexpected night.
No verbiage but something much softer—

the umbrella of a dark crane, its whole
wingspan covering any small rip in the sky,

as a sleepless man rises, writes letters
to release himself from the dwelling
of the past, his lost children,

a strange peace gathering
in the fulcrum where they fade.

When he returns to where we lay,
the odd spaces fill with portals of black
or evergreen, some glimmer golden
as if the end of a lit wick floods in wax.

There in a quiet theatre, we learn again.

Between

Our hips,

corridors, open rivers.

Quiet animals come close,

lean into each other.

Between One P.M. & Four

As if in a sudden shower of flames,
flowers drift from the pomegranate.

A crimson pillow falls from the bed.
His shoulder cramps up.

The room has filled with guitars.
They lean into each other,

familiar many-colored instruments
playing songs about our distant

& recent lives, as intertwined now
hip to hip, canyons open &

quietly daring, we come close
like animals with such careful intent.

From the chalky widening landscapes—
we hear that timeless innate growl.

The blue river of veins
in his neck is a map of pulsing

bloodlines, a cure for the center—
for what seemed lifeless. A river

flows there too, washing away

what is no longer necessary.

Music

Your fingers stagger

to a stained light

you remember.

Listen.

Go inside.

Unzip the deep thrum,

the luminous spine.

Old Music

When you remembered to listen,
you searched for a room
with good acoustics, vaulted ceiling:

in the air a woman's sighs,
the swish of orchid organza,
the lyric notes of the flesh.

At the end of the street,
high waves jump the sea wall.

You go inside.
You're told to play the bass guitar,
lean it back against your ribs
like your lost widow

O then rock her in your arms
until a stained light wounds
your forehead & your hollowness,

until your fingers stagger,
drunken dancers too luminous
to know they're no longer young.

The deep thrum on the strings is your skin.
The tango is complicated by our differences.
Play. Dance across the broken black,
the white tiles, blazing . . .

But it is always (I place one white camellia
behind each ear) too quick to have been real—

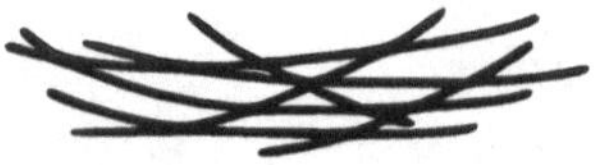

the subtle cradle of hip in hip,
the weeping silk slip as it hits
the floor—this coal in the limbs
is a bitter smoke. You ask me for water.

I give you rum,
say *unzip me slowly.*
The spine will instruct the mouth.
The mouth speaks of salt & of death.

I am ruined.

Chorale

I no longer quite gleam,

have a weakness

for the storm

the beautiful curves,

& scratches of beginnings—

Operas can't be tidy.

Neptune Chorale

I have always had a weakness
for beautiful dresses of flora—

dusky silks, eyelet cottons—
a closet of cravings
no longer needed.

The floors have grown
so hard tonight, doorknobs
gleam pewter & stormy
as if to say *age can't be tidy.*

Your face—a planet
above me in a lake of night.

Rare rain scores the roof,
curves & scratches against
the windows but I've
drawn a strange horizon.

The storm can't get inside
the ring of beginning—

where we have time,
we still have
a little time left.

Tiny Spears

Antique vistas

smear all the hills.

We could be anywhere.

But we're going

anyhow,

howling.

And Both of Us Saw Tiny Spears of Violets

He is red ripples
on the gentle hills.
Undulations
of antique vistas.
A sky of winter.
An almost spring sky.
Next season.
Then to the next.
We might lose our way,
may fail, but we're going
anyhow, towards blossoms
cascaded over the castings
of the hills. As if smeared.
As if scattered. Moments
you can't make up.
I never had sweet dreams.
But this one is. And sure,
I know one should not
remove the wooden stake
from the frozen heart,
we're risking total
collapse, but, fuck it,
we do it anyhow. Threads
of violets release from the throats
of all involved in a kind of howling
that's bearable, as if a curse
has been lifted. Not everything
has to be lovely, yet this is.
There is ruby all over
the landscape. We could be

anywhere. It doesn't matter
who thinks what.
We are home because
we wake up & we say so.

Netsuke

Tied, clasped & wed—

two figures

recall

the land spirits hiding

in the stone-gray pool.

The old bones thunder.

Netsuke Gradually Waking

And in the morning
a warm sculpture—

two figures cocoon
in a single form

our bodies beyond
the lathe of the years,
clasped & wed

before land spirits
hide from the sun,

when the peach tulips
are still sealed against
the cold shapes of night,

before the young redtail
bathes in the gray stone pool,

before hunger stirs
& you brew the coffee,
while I clean the room,

before sunrise cracks in
hotly wired, before we yield

to the thundering city—
& we know we can't live apart

from the sea & we don't
or far from the trees & we don't,

before wide awake
we must go our separate ways.

Woman Leaning

In our house

an orchard,

nearly disappeared,

is peeking through

reciting a myth.

Woman Leaning Over a Resting Man Reciting a Myth

We look alike, don't you agree?
No, no, you say, but still, we do—
around the eyes, golden lions roaming
into fire, licking, & a third eye,

secretive on your forehead, grants us
permission to refrain from repeating
old blunders; your irises—ore, gilded
eggs, shells un-cracked—& of course

I was no virgin when we met
but was still completely whole,
& *admit it, it's like looking in a mirror,*
you must agree! But *no, no,* you insist

you get to play the hairy bear,
contend that I, I am exquisite & I, I
say *yes, ok, then we are both beast & beauty,*
constant as a once-forgotten fairytale

forest where two swans might entwine
as one, where a childhood tale comes true,
where dogwood & lilies peek through
a creaking gate & beyond that,

an orchard, where we can come to rest
& warm a god in our house. Call it
the mad dance, call it that ringing
in the ears always present,

those bells of recognition.

After Brigit Pegeen Kelly

God

The coastal mists

    from the underworld

fling themselves

    over the rooftops.

A Wounded God Dressed in Brocade

After three days we entered the coastal mists
hunting wild poppies, lupine, fiddleneck

with their sturdy rooster crowns crooked
as if courting mysteries from the underworld.

And yes, maybe some seeds drowned in rains
so dense even city birds had been too sodden

to throw themselves from the rooftops.
And yes, someone got sick, but not too badly.

Someone got drunk but was driven safely home.
Some left hand-written notes on simple moments—

he was a sylph, a stag magnificent & vulnerable.
Later there was the thought to make love

unseen under the drooping skirts of the saturated
old oaks, chartreuse with brightened growth,

where we could fold a timeline of years
into a small book of burnished mementos,

each begging to be touched just one last time
before being mulched into a sonic cavalcade

of bells, bells, bells, bells.
Weddings are just like that—

the way we call to each other.
The way we are answered.

HE CARRIES ME LIKE
A BOUQUET OF
FLOWERS

The word in the middle of the body. The word in the closed eye.
The word in the road, almost stepped on but seen at the
last minute, put in a pocket like a fallen leaf.

—Holly Prado

Lizards

You're

all the beautiful boys

swimming the rapids

never fucked too pink

honey crisp

nude at first light

when the birds talk

to the trees.

Lizards Are Always Dreaming

You're all the beautiful boys
of youth lying like lizards
on the granite grottos, warm & tan,
the boys I never fucked, too pink
& plump to be what they desired.

You're honey crisp, not melancholy,
so yes, I leapt over dread,
in my worn-out shoes,
still good enough to go.

You're not afraid
of the lakeside charnel
grounds in the cottonwood
grove crumbled with drought,
scarlet foxgloves bent & thirsty,
where I scattered my dead,
danced nude on their graves
as a fisherman came
with first light, threw out
his line, never even saw me.

But you see & we listen
as birds talk to the trees,
who talk to wolves
who tell us their secrets.

You are every beautiful boy
of my youth—supple, easy,
loose-muscled after swimming
the rapids, & I, composed,
dress in blood red to bring you
baskets of stars, every last
one of them exploding.

Overflowing

We buried the masks.

Glass angels

everywhere

wrote instructions on

chronic pain.

Your children

were

building amulets.

The Room Overflowing with Tulips

After we burned
the Christmas tree
dangerously close
to the house;
after the New Year
when the neighbor
kept delivering foil-wrapped
seasonal chocolates,
root-infused teas
for chronic pain;
after your children grew
limbs of silence
that broke off; when
adornments, glued heirlooms,
glass birds & window angels,
were wrapped & carefully
stored; when we realized
your children would never call—
we buried the masks,
we buried three more,
we conducted the amputations;
the dulled hatchet we used
on the tree got lost
in the grass; we handwrote
instructions on building amulets—
used the correct poisons
to kill off the useless;
translated the vague jazz
of sorrow & you covered me
where I lay & I covered you
where you lay, the hours
everywhere, tulips everywhere.

At All Hours

This summer we dream ravens.

Inertia

drips over my skin.

The hourglass in my throat

fills with the waters we are.

Summoned to Perform at All Hours of the Night

It's so late I can hear my grandmother,
Margery, slap an ace-high straight down
on linoleum, light a Doral, become smoke.

We are so wet again, our pool hair swims
across cushions. Is it fever or is it sex?

The hum of a large horse fly scrolls
illegibly on the ceiling. Sleep fills
with ravens, their shattering blackness

mocks my inertia & yes, it's far
too costly to fly anywhere, so
this summer we travel in dreams.

The hourglass in my throat tells me
time is running out as my dead
grandmother stands like a mummy
drinking red wine at her kitchen sink.

She shifts weight to relieve bone spurs—
wills me her name, her cravings
& hunchback, goads me to love
glitter & gore in equal measure.

I light a candle, fix her in silhouettes
that drip over my skin.

You smell so good even fast asleep,
your eyes tumbling like the unborn
under lids crisscrossed with lilac streams—

the waters we come from. The waters we are.
Margery, you call me & no one else ever has.

Tiptoeing

Between

both horizons

affection sees only my red lipstick.

Tiptoeing

When you lay your head between
my breasts you're always whistling,

seeing only rosy mountains.

Sometimes it's just a matter of momentum,
skirting what can't bear close examination.

Midsummer is behind us—a leaping wild fox.

Go ahead & holler off-key. My red
lipstick dispels a lot.

I too pray not to panic at the moment of death.

We align ourselves with both horizons,

two jeweled birds who whip
a filthy puddle into rainbow pinwheels.

Come close to me my love, close as you can.

When you get here
I will make you something nice.

After Ralph Angel

Always

The daylight arrives.

My hands are

a giant groundswell.

I run my fingers over

oracles.

We are

imperfect

in our skin.

Ancient Is Always

Look how my hands are steady,
not a shake yet, no tremor.

The daylight arrives, reads the abacus,
the eras behind are pentimenti.

We are always almost old until we are,
in our personal, imperfect homes of skin.

So, I protect this shared hydrangea bed
where I count your vertebra as if casting

oracle runes, running my fingers
over ancestral landmasses of yarrow,

goldenrod, where once you were a bearded god—
a giant groundswell, my fighting companion,

with unassailable perfect teeth & baritone growls.
But now my gait, slower with my black oak cane

ensures I won't bellow, won't win
the always war, neither will you, nobody does.

The Sea

She is a needle

crossing

the blank page,

a pillar of black salt—

skirts

billowed

in a wilderness—

the future a coin.

Into the Sea

From space the man is a needle,
threading the architecture of waves—

like a compass he tracks the blue line,
then the woman on shore—

he knows where she is billowed
in black skirts—a woman

not a pillar of salt, not a heron's roost
but the open eye of the season,

she tracks the man in the swirl of wilderness,

measures every incline, every tower of wave
he might climb like a spider crossing a blank page—

she knows where he is—
the specific slope of his shoulders as he tosses

the future like a coin onto the rising peaks,
each liquid cliff a shifting story, which, no matter what

he will crave & she wants everything
that washes up to her feet, broken or whole,

gray on gray, cloud phantoms too
as fishermen come with their nets to stand ready,

while she blows the spider back into the crackle of dawn.

Sunlight

It's not selfish

to be

sliced with sunset.

We decipher our way

cast in liquid gold.

Late Sunlight like Monet

Searching for gilded snowmelt ponds
shrouded in the woods,

we decipher our way

over the decaying storm fall
hidden in dense lodgepole pines.

Sliced with sunset,
there are so many hidden

sides of things:

fire on the oceans behind us,

the cries of gulls
spiraling updrafts,

amber clouds too

as if clouds could burn
all regrets away.

No, it's not selfish to push,
to mount sundown, strip beside

you & enter the opal water—
cast in liquid gold—

no remorse.

Chimes

My red cup balances

in the dirt.

Yellow roses

vine the morning,

claw

through old scars.

Caught

in some invisible

airstream,

the sun crests the roofline,

alive.

So What if the Chimes Are Silent?

It is Sunday. Look how the tiny
unnamed brown birds in the pomegranate
shudder, so small they'd fit together
in my palms, yet they shake the entire tree.

See how the shady side of the fountain
has gathered moss so thick it might be
clay one could mold into a strong vessel.

It's always a surprise, how the yellow rose
vines rise from barren root,
claw, thorn & bud over the neighbor's wall,
(the one who's never liked me)
until flowers consume the redwood fence

the way you wrap around me
& together we become an original
carved from old scars. My red
cup balances in the dirt, steam weaves
from coffee in the orbit of morning.

You quietly play the crooked guitar
so don't see me point to a knot of seagulls
crossing the split-open nectarine clouds,

spider webs loosely drifting through
the budding red maple until the gulls
part into three, unite, part, unite
again, caught in some invisible airstream,

the way prayer sounds into & through,
the way just sitting with you in
the dawn & plaiting your hair seems
everything one needs to stay alive.

EXTINCTION

It was almost dark, and they could smell the air that came
towards them over the water of the pokuna, could hear
the rustling of unseen creatures.

—Michael Ondaatje

Ashes

Signals travel

back & forth

between

oaks,

birches—

between

all the departed,

netting the globe.

They shine.

Talking to Ashes

They are golden so it must be tomorrow.
Under a tree of dreamcatchers,
the drought cracks oaks in Topanga—
Oregon suffocates in smoke,
hydrangeas and birches burn.

The trees are uncorrupted in union,
in communion/ interspecies, carbon-fed,
with sunlight they give birth to violins.

While four chainsaws tear the tall eucalyptus
across the street to rags, my index & ring
fingers bend over my thumb like a mother
protecting a babe—the gesture had *been* my mother's.

The last of the family line, I carry the horned
spine of my grandmother's bundle so I live
in both under and over worlds where signals
travel from root to root, netting the globe.

Debris flies the way grasshoppers do. Sawdust
coats the sunlight like the marigold blooms
covering graves on the Day of the Dead, as
destiny's candles shine signals back & forth

between all the departed. So, I ask them
to remember me, show me the way,
when I too return to the entrance.

Elegy

No water—

falling from blind eyes,

the blackened

corpses of the trees.

I can hear

the dry wind—

Orchard Elegy

The blackened corpses in the oldest
almond groves of the great valley

lie uprooted, hissing
as they heave their sap—

the farmland topsoil, blown away,
ends the tumbled ballets

of pink springtime almond blossoms.

The rune of constraint has two lines—
the same backwards & forwards.

And there's no way out, no water,
only blood because like dry wind

that ties the seasons in knots,
we won't stop warring, won't stop

screaming like children who've
not yet been taught never

to step on the bees falling
from the blind sky instead of rain.

I can hear the dead.

On Fire

The trees smell blood.

The journals of smoke

stammer

onto the last

of the moon.

Your hands shimmer.

No One Dreams We Are on Fire

Alive & cold, wet grass, stones
on our feet, we take up

our journals of smoke.

Another war because someone
wants what others have.

Snakes shimmer up my arms
as I try by firelight to resume

the exam of living in the face
of so much gore—

someone wants to paint the stars black.

None of us can correctly
imagine what other lives are like.

Even thousands of miles away
the trees smell blood, try to warn us.

The chronicles stammer on.
The day. The date. The year.

The last of the moon lies on her back
tethered helplessly to the sun.

Our outlines smear into each other.

Your hands are made of every husband.

Clasped together, our hands
are made of everyone.

Covid

A sudden shock

of winter

in my ribs.

I am

a bad temper, no face.

But love mounts the waves,

in one flash—

a choir

of pure perfection.

A Covid Christmas Card

Last night I had a bad temper
& no face. At daybreak
my love runs to the ocean,
weaves under, over, under,
through the waves, a choir
of pelicans overhead.
A dog chases surf.
The tide rises to a sandcastle's
apex, floods the moat then
the structure.

Last night I had bright
chest pain—crushed blood
cherries in my ribs.
This is a winter of terror
& grief. I am a cut-out doll
against the sky. A landscape
of storm creeps in. My love
mounts the swells, surfs little
slices of feigned immortality.

Last night I had blooms
then petals, lungs full
of peonies flying loose lifted me
off the mattress in bits
of collage paper torn from
newspaper clippings, headlines,
the doctor named "never," dark
banks of thunder in my ribs.

Last night I had a lavish cloud—
but this morning my love stands
easy on a Christmas-red board &
freezing, rides one flash of
pure perfection. We may live
in the vault year but the sea
never conforms. I bury my legs
in cold sand. A sudden shock
of sunlight on my neck is a shawl.

Wolves

Still just simple children

we uncover caches

of nightmares.

Stolen

light

whispers

in the aftermath.

Stone Wolves

Waking afraid, we stagger
to the roadway,
& as if we're both
still simple children,

we embrace in the spotlight
of streetlamp. Our nightrobes
whisper against our skin,
as we offer incantations

to ward off the caches
of blue ghosts streaming around
the globe ensnared in nightmares.

In the aftermath of their furious shadows,
we see the world is already ash.

Five planets align on the glass
night, their light threadbare. Still,
the firmament absorbs everything.

So we will believe it could forgive us
for having made love to stone wolves.

Biography

In small collections

of ruthlessness—

eruptions

of blue light,

I thrash.

Our hair grows

white

in the news cycle.

You Need to Get Over Your Biography

Across the street, a new baby
shrieks, angry in its new body.

My collarbones hurt. I thrash around,
can't get the blue light to shut down
the news cycles, the collective stupor.

In the insect moan of the city,
the tiny gutters of my backbone
fit to my love's as he plays guitar.
I listen for translation.
Our hair grows white silently.

Some days I am crippled
just watching the razors
of hummingbirds aim at victory
over hunger in small eruptions
of ruthlessness,

the way a man might chance
to shoot a clay pigeon
out of the sky at just such
an angle each dense speckle
utterly disappears.

Sealed

Cloaked in

purple wildfire smoke,

we forget the exits,

stare out the windows

at cloud houses of survival

marked by teeth.

Some wanted every inch.

The Earth Then Sealed

We fly above a patchwork cloaked with purple
wildfire smoke, topographies erased.
We fly over the flat plains to the breadbasket
belly where rivers once flowed before the sky
froze, dried the earth then sealed it,
eyes sewn shut, soil blown off
in the terrors of our new weather.

We fly over the land where my parents
courted (what is that town down there?)
as if the *Will you marry me* myth magically
transforms to the lasting stewardship of love.

We fly over the blue ridge, the protest dirges
of coal miner bones reaching up deep shafts,
where corporate opium ripped my brother from
this world. We fly over my beloved's mother, sealed in
a carriage house of survival, those places we store
our elders while they wait for their Big Moment.

We fly over what's seen but we've forgotten—
Lake Erie, the shriveled blue of a failed
essential organ masked under evaporation fogs.
We fly above highways & train tracks, every
crossroad marked with skulls & bones—
the dinosaur teeth of untamed terrains gone.

We fly through cloud-houses above violence
where every town is starved for rain.
Some believed it was all theirs to claim,
trees & boulders in measured cages of barbwire.

We fly over our ancestral graves. Over
our own spectral lives. We stare out
the windows & wish we could fly backwards,
searching for any point we could turn it around.

No one can locate the drop-offs, the exits.
So we wait for the Big Moment together.
We will not have long to wait.

Monster

The white mound.

The books of

untended years.

Under those lace dreams—

god or something.

I can touch things

you would not believe.

Monster Considered

Thinking of god or something
down on the ground here, I admit
there is a monster in me.

She lives in the dank under layers
of silt, sloughed from untended years
like old skin, petrified, surrounded

by choirs of porcelain figurines,
little tableaus of memories & ambitions,
a company of still lives, perfect

as a stage set inside a snow-globe,
the collected works of parasols,
flounced hoop skirts, hiding

the handiwork of time,
& under those lace dreams,
a white burial mound I can touch,

flocks of tattered butterflies,
books of unused disintegrated
parchments. The monster flows

over the arms of the chair, powerless
against creeping seasonlessness.
There are things I think &

you don't want to know,
things I have sometimes done.
You would not believe what is in here.

Pain

I made you

a wonderful box

the exact size of

my favorite fable.

In all salutations,

you visit faithfully.

You follow me,

never drool.

You're the one on one

no one can name.

Ask anyone.

Dear Pain,

My favorite fable at five was to ride a magic carpet into ciphered expansions of outer space, dragged by two huge saucer-eyed mastiffs who never drooled but instead hummed Gregorian chants. Dear pain, you live out there too in the black hole, you're that loud bird we all watch soar overhead. The one no one can name but everyone remembers when it blasts into a window only to rise again & fly. Never a captured creature, we meet you at the threshold of gravity which you eschew. Accomplished at all sorts of shapeshifts, you deserve an altar, a TV show, a hand-painted plate at every table. You live in all goodbyes & salutations. You visit our skeletons faithfully. Ask anyone on any street. Nobody likes a constant dervish wind, but we've gotten to know you, expect your explosive precision on every hard surface—it's just the nature of figure to ground— the way of things. So, dear pain, I made you a wonderful box the exact size of my body. Adorned with every possible color & glyph, I open it each day to hear your fresh soliloquy, new composition, or at least a unique version of yesterday's tune. You're always pretty lively, good for a date. Can I call you bff, since you follow me all over the place, to the corner store for wine, the bathroom, washing the dishes, down & up the stairs— clump-clump. Over every molten hour you adorn me, kiss me, caress me, cradle me. I know you'll never leave me alone. So, why don't we just go ahead, why don't we get married.

Extinction

Ten folded

stories

crack the glass,

fascinated by their own mirages.

In a recording

I speak out loud,

irate & not hidden

anymore.

Extinction: The Woman in the Box

The woman in the box is speaking.
I am the woman in the box.
I hear a staircase to an old season.

The archives are a red neon door
left in blankets of dreamy ficus tangles.
I am the woman with the claws.

My belly is made of ten folded
stories too big to fit in the box.
Even truths can be frozen by narrow

judgments. Wednesday, leaf
hornets crack the glass,
fascinated by their own mirages.

I am the woman who does not want
to plod up to see the dead oaks,
their trunks collapsing after

the fires, or watch the canyons
erode while coyotes run
the middle line of sunset,

bristling with irate thirst.
I am the woman who is not hidden
anymore in a tent that doesn't

fully protect from stinging ants.
In a recording, a modern Buddha
says, all life is shiny, a little plastic

toy you better not step on.
In the dark I speak out loud, ask
how long my heart intends to beat,

ask what did we do, what do we do?

Empathy

This vision

is a blood tattoo.

In the distance

the point of gravity is a

smokescreen,

an x-ray.

Oh souvenir of a baby bird—

echo the quiet chill of the real life

I can never

restore.

Empathy Drawn on Asphalt

This must be how mother felt—
a small fragile world of swollen legs,
fissures in vertebrae, crumbled cervical,
thoracic, coccyx, osteo landslide
dissolved to the lowest point of gravity,
the unclear vision, waking up
to hillocks of flesh static within
her mountain home, stratus clouds
heavily clinging to topsoil, veils over
the view of the elaborate tulle of the sea.

This must be how mother felt
and envious too at times,
with her unfulfilled visions
of families at tables with fat turkeys,
board games, candles splashing
homey light, domestically happy
without the frozen distances
of long-brewed anger, resentments,
the injuries & subtle struggles for control.

And perhaps this is how she felt
as my brother, still just a child,
stared at her body with jeering
disgust, maybe a smokescreen
for longing or lust, but sneering
nonetheless at her shape, her skin,
her varicose veins, backlogged canals
of blood tattoos she bore from carrying,
first him, then me—my sole sibling,
who died alone in West Virginia

in a trailer park, transformed by death
to an oxycodone pool of jelly on the floor,
twenty guns in the safe, surrounded
by the unseen, unshared tenderness
of his own exquisite art.

My morning this morning might echo
one of mother's, waking bewildered,
altered, vulnerable as an infant solo
in a crib, slowly unclutching legs,
knees, hips, ten fingers, scanning
memory's inventory, to recall how once
in angry impatience I'd grabbed her wrist
too hard as she'd tried to turn the stubborn
knob of my old gas stove—her arm
like a thin neck, delicate as a baby bird.

This must be how my mother felt
when she learned she'd go deaf,
the same quiet chill I felt when my third
surgeon's face fell as he surveyed the x-rays,
then me sitting on his table in my firm
young yogini limbs, with no clue at all
of the distance between an idea & real life.

This must be how mother felt
walking the woods on her island,
each hard step of my slow pace downhill
a souvenir of her steps as my morning course
is crossed by cheerful tan runners swarming
past in packs, then two young men

with their new digital cameras sneaking
a shot—because, sure, I'm curious
with my black oak cane, oversized hat,
red lipstick, slight limp, with my long white hair,
always looking down to watch where I'm going—
of course, they had to sneak a few shots,
to which I had to say, *I know you've just stolen
my image* & he tries to explain, but I already get it
so I don't demand a deletion, because yes,
he could destroy the shot, but the action can't
be reversed or returned as I can never restore
her to me, to brush her hair, make chamomile tea,
scramble her eggs & tell her at least
one last time, I am so very,
so very, very sorry.

In a Mirror

Upstairs in a mirror,

perfectly stunned,

a tasseled

woman with winter hair

watches

a bird

evaporate in the fog.

Earthworms rise.

A Leaf, a Lagoon in a Mirror/
Catskills Autumnal

A scribble of moon falls
through leaf-shiver,
spun on silver threads,
a twirl of brightness
perfectly dizzy
with the harvest embrace
of ghost light. Naked
birch strips off its gold.

A white horse clops,
slow as chilled syrup,
not a truck in sight
on the blacktop.
Upstairs in the mirror,
a blue woman tasseled
with winter hair
hums a love song
before the snow comes.
Downstairs a boy
in his crown of stars
builds the future
in blocks with letters.

Through auburn curls
& verbiage, the boy
watches a balloon
become a bird
that evaporates into
the fog of minutes.
The perfume of soil,

dirt clods, earth worms
rises. Behind him
the clock in the hall
so loud, winds back & forth
like a lover unable
to leave, weaving
both together, at last.

The Oceans

The floating

indigo mountains

are not words.

The tunnel is red.

You check your watch,

glimpse a child pulsing out

of the black highway.

Fate is a fingerprint.

Hold on.

From the Mountains to the Prairies to the Oceans White With Foam

—Irving Berlin 1918

My mother comes out of the darkness.
The tunnel is red, is opening, closing
like a wild poppy tracking day into night.
Under the floating indigo mountains,
there are no words, just this act as she pulses out
with her mother's black & white checkered apron
tied around her, sagging slightly as if the pockets
are full of peanuts or keys & she intends something.
I know this since her lips are moving—not unlike
a silent player piano in an empty formal dining room,
the table set with tarnished silver, no, there's no
discernable sound, only a slight murmur
from the diagrams of history's shadows—
too many to count flinging from her chest
as she steps onto the black highway.

You check your watch to see where you are standing.
The sound is everywhere without sound, like a lie
you can glimpse, like a city of ether yet built of solids,
of minerals, of soils. We are running out of sand.
A child in another time shrieks, *everybody, don't see me!*
stridently, over & over. What will become of us
we wonder & search for each other's hands, closing
our fingers around one another like wild red poppies
clinging as we watch the indigo peaks fade.

There is a small deer at the edge of the copse
that has burrowed through the blackberry hedge
following a tunnel carved into the bramble wall

by many years of animals leading one another
to the ragged border of the cottonwoods, that maze
now winter-bare behind the doe, who sniffs
the water-laden atmosphere startling only slightly
as a car sluices past speeding on the wounded spine
of asphalt & she finds nothing new under
the pewter sun, just a humming, a dappling.

My mother swells like roses in her bell white gown,
turns on the bathroom light & never returns.
Bells ring in cathedrals & dells everywhere at once,
calling out the names of immense stones sawn in half,
ancestries etched in every single tone. As we watch her go,
no one calls out, calls her back—we do not dare startle
the veils—our breath like sleds gliding so tenderly
over the air that opens the seams of the earth invisibly.
We hear a dog in the distance squeal in some sort of terror
or pain but we cannot reach out to comb its coat
gently with our palms. We have to hold on.
There seems no other way, or regret might gather
in a sea of black pebbles filling our throats & genitals.

Frozen, we bear witness as the indigo mountains
are carried away in the beaks of so many crows
like memories of something pure, truthful, until
the sky becomes a bed of spilled ink, a babbling roar,
drowning, not brave & costly like all true freedoms.
Goodbye, we wave to the saturated peaks, as the doe
comes to stand beside us, staring at our locked hands,
then our wet feet covered in sticks & mud, then
at our faces—searching our eyes as if asking what color

fate is, asking like a fingerprint, or music. She studies,
wearing the same wordlessly quizzical look
I'd last seen my mother wear when in the island house
she'd come to kneel with great pain at my side where
I'd slept on the floor near the fire & whispered,
Did you do the right thing? Do you still believe
that's true? Then the kettle was screaming, which
simply meant it was time to go.

NOTES

With slight variations, the following lines come from solstice collaborative writing practices with the High Priestesses of Poetry group: "you need to get over your biography" and "the hourglass in my throat," ahuva s. zaslavsky; "Summoned to perform at all hours of the night" and "glitter & dirt in equal measure," Andra Vltavin.

The title of the poem "A Wounded God Dressed in Brocade," and the line "a sylph, a stag magnificent & vulnerable," were taken from a beautiful note sent to me by Marsha de la O.

The line "A god in our house" is taken from the title of the anthology *A God in the House* (Kaminsky & Towler 2012).

The epigraphs are from the following books: Holly Prado, *These Mirrors Prove It* (Cahuenga Press 2004); Michael Ondaatje, *Anil's Ghost* (McClelland and Stewart 2000).

"Imagoes, Minerals" is playing with the correlation between the stages of development in insects that have survived to the "pupa" (3d stage) and achieve the final "imago" (4th stage) phase. In psychoanalytic parlance, the word "imago" originated with Carl Jung to describe the state of human development "situated between the conscious and unconscious" becoming in a sense "a chiaroscuro, a partially autonomous complex not fully integrated into consciousness, and therefore still infused with the mythical figures of the collective…" (close paraphrase of Jung from *Man and His Symbols*, 1964).

"Old Music" was inspired by the triumphant resurrection of the Buena Vista Social Club, which was rediscovered and shepherded back into success by Ry Cooder, as shown in the 1999 Wim Wenders film of the same name.

"Neptune Chorale" was written under the spell of the "The Flower Duet" by Leo Delibes (Lakme, 1883).

"And Both of Us Saw Tiny Spears of Violets" is an ekphrastic poem loosely based on Christo and Jeanne-Claude's yellow umbrella installations in Gorman, California, and Ibaraki, Japan, opened simultaneously at sunrise by 1880 workers on October 9, 1991.

"Netsuke Gradually Waking" takes its imagery from the Japanese Netsuke, which are small sculptures, frequently of animals, musicians, and couples in various erotic embraces.

"Woman Leaning Over a Resting Man Reciting a Myth" is a pale but earnest homage to the brilliant poet Brigit Pegeen Kelly and her masterwork "The Orchard." It also nods to many familiar fairytales involving swans, beauties, and beasts, whose qualities are those of adult sexuality and the underworlds.

"Tiptoeing" has the hope of borrowing its tone from Ralph Angel, who taught me, in some mysteriously unexplicit way, how make a book from a mess of poems.

"Ancient Is Always" has a reference to Runes, which were developed by Germanic tribes as an alphabet dating to ca 150CE. They were likely derived from Roman Latin. In modernity, they are a divination tool made of small stones etched with symbols.

"Talking to Ashes" takes a core image from the Mexican festival the Day of the Dead, when families gather after nightfall to picnic on the graves of the departed, feasting on all the favorite foods of the dead as a way of maintaining good relations. The poem was drafted in a free-write session with ash good and is for her.

"No One Dreams We Are on Fire" and "Stone Wolves" are both dedicated to all who are living in active warzones.

"Extinction: The Woman in the Box" was written in response to the increase in California wildfires and global warming. It also owes gratitude to Dhamma teacher, Thanisarro Bikkhu of the Metta Forest Monastery.

"From the Mountains to the Prairies to the Oceans White with Foam" is a line taken from Irving Berlin's "God Bless America," the copyright to which was eventually signed over to the Boy Scouts of America and Girl Scouts of the USA.

ACKNOWLEDGMENTS

I am very grateful to the following publications for accepting my work, sometimes in earlier versions.

"Extinction" & "Extinction: The Woman in the Box"—*Bicoastal Review*, 2024
"At All Hours" & "Summoned to Perform at All Hours of the Night"
    —*Cleaver*, 2024
"Overflowing" & "The Room Overflowing with Tulips"—*Passionfruit*, 2024
"Ashes" & "Talking to Ashes"—*Catamaran*, 2024
"Empathy," "Empathy Drawn on Asphalt," "Fire," "No One Dreams We
    Are on Fire," "Sealed" & "The Earth Then Sealed" (published as
    "We Fly Over")—*Interlitq*, Issue 6, 2023
"So What if The Chimes Are Silent?"—*Spillway*, 2021
"From the Mountains to the Prairies to the Oceans White With Foam"
    —*Hotel Amerika*, 2020
"Old Music"—*Spillway*, 2018

As is true for all collections of poetry, this one could not have been made without the community of fellow poets, artists & beloveds I am blessed to know. So much gratitude to my first readers & frequent collaborators, Celeste Goyer, James Cushing, ash good & the poets in the Monday night workshop—Marjorie Becker, Jan Wesley, Brenda Yates, Jim Natal, Jeanette Clough, Dina Hardy, Paul Lieber, Mariano Zaro & my trusted reader, Sarah Maclay. So much gratitude to David St. John, Judith Pacht, Marsha de la O, Phil Taggart, Ralph Angel,

Susan Terris, Michelle Bitting. I owe a big thank you to the Portland Solstice writing group for so many inspirations. To the fearless publishers, writers & editors at Giant Claw—the brilliant poet Gail Wronsky & novelist Chuck Rosenthal—thank you! To Alan Davis at New Rivers Press, the people at What Books Press, Red Hen Press & Tebot Bach—I am so grateful for your camaraderie, your work & your support. To the stewards of Beyond Baroque—Richard Modiano, Fred Dewey, Quentin Ring, Jimmy Vega and the new generations—thank you all! I have been given so much by Brett Hall & the committed people at the Community of Writers—C.D. Wright whose friendship was so meaningful for me as a person & a writer, Robert Hass, Forrest Gander, Sharon Olds, Dean Young, I am grateful for your inspiration & for your kindness. To the beloved Holly Prado, I will always be in debt. Her respect was & is profoundly meaningful in sustaining me. Deep bows to Harry Northup, Phoebe MacAdams, Cecilia Woloch, Brendan Constantine, Friday Gretchen. The list of people to whom I owe a real debt is long. Forgive any omissions. I carry the imprints of all of you, your teachings, poems, friendships. I offer my inexpressible love to Dr. Erna Osterweil whose rare skills, strength & humanity saved my life as well as to my lifelong running mates, Lilly Dale Reed, Cristina Lopez, Sudie Shipman, Mary Angel, Connie Call, Katherine Williams, again to Sarah Maclay, Judith Pacht, Celeste Goyer, James Cushing & ash good! Finally, thank you my love, Adrian Baer, for giving up so many vacations so I can make poems & books.

HOLADAY MASON is the author of five previous collections of poetry—*Towards the Forest, Dissolve, The Red Bowl: A Fable in Poems, The "She" Series: A Venice Correspondence* (with Sarah Maclay), and *The Weaver's Body*—as well as two chapbooks—*Interlude* & *Light Spilling From its Own Cup*. Nominated for multiple Pushcart prizes, publications include *Hotel Amerika, Spillway, Solo, Pool, Poetry International, The Laurel Review* & more. Co-editor for Beyond Baroque's anthology *Echo 681,* where she has also led writing workshops, she is currently poetry editor for online art & poetry magazine *Furious Pure* and was previously poetry editor for *Mental Shoes*. A portrait & fine art photographer focusing on the surreal nature of beauty and humans as a part of nature, she has been in private practice as a psychotherapist since 1993. Ms. Mason lives in Venice California with a mean-ass cat named Ms. T.T. (AKA Ms. Twirly Tail), a big ol' dog named Chewie & her husband, the musician and educator Adrian Baer (#jellybirdla). She can be found at www.holadaymason.com.

www.ingramcontent.com/pod-product-compliance
Lightning Source LLC
Chambersburg PA
CBHW050857150626
46549CB00013B/2676

* 9 7 9 8 9 9 0 0 1 4 9 2 3 *